Tanka Quartets

Autumn Noelle Hall

&

David C. Rice

Published by Just Keep Walking Press

Berkeley, California

ISBN: 978-1-7331154-1-4

Library of Congress Control Number: 2020915351

Printed by Lulu.com

*For Gary, who recognizes poetry as soul work
and gifts me the time to write.*

For my family

"You cannot get through a single day without having an impact on the world around you. What you do makes a difference, and you have to decide what kind of difference you want to make."
—Jane Goodall

" . . . for the growing good of the world is partly dependent on unhistoric acts; and that things are not so ill with you and me as they might have been, is half owing to the number who lived faithfully a hidden life, and rest in unvisited tombs."
—George Eliot, *Middlemarch*

praise all solitary artists
adding layers to meaning
I also like to linger
in the responsive wing
still under construction

collaboration—
many hands created
the Sistine Chapel
heavenly, to have painted
even one patch of that sky

we're all lumps of clay—
when someone else gives us
breath
we don't have to be
our own god

not takers
but leavers along this path . . .
balanced cairns
of four stones each
waymarkers for those to come

Table of Contents

Introduction

Autumn: While I've never asked David why it was he initially invited me to write with him, I'm pretty sure it had something to do with birds. We are both avid watchers, feeders and fans of any and all feathered friends. What began for me as an avian way to avoid closing clichés (such as Best or Regards), ended up becoming a routine part of our correspondence. To this day, we still sign off with our latest sightings: "Stellar's Jay on the black oil seed Saturday, Autumn" or "Maybe a Merganser Monday, David." This birdbrained notion somehow led first to more in-depth correspondence, then an unexpected opportunity to edit tanka prose for Ribbons, and eventually to these four-tanka sequences, which we came to call Connects.

David had a lot of ideas about how best to Connect—and (I hope he'll forgive me for mentioning this) a lot of rules. Each of the tanka needed to link to the one before by more than just an image, word or syntax. The last of the four needed to somehow tie back to the first. We needed to avoid too many "ing" endings. As David shared them with me, I compiled a list of what he deemed "mostly banned words": heart, soul, dream, beauty, love, along with abstract ideas like kindness, patience, compassion (about which David recommended we, "Convey these concepts through imagery; however, connect through the concepts, not just the imagery"). For a life-long rule-bender like me, it was a tall order!

But then, I do relish a challenge; and more importantly, I really like David—and I admire his love of nature as much as his spirited work. So, over the course of a year, give or take, we proceeded to write some 260 tanka each to form 130 Connects together. This collection comprises the best of those sequences, which, because they play a little like longer songs made up of tanka's short songs as they harmonize, I thought we might call Quartets. I hope that you will enjoy reading them—if you listen closely, you might even hear birdcalls in the background.

David: When younger, we want to see what we can accomplish. At mid-life, getting to know ourselves becomes important. In the background, though, softly from our beginnings and increasingly louder as we age, is the desire to have what a friend of mine calls "a relational life."

Western poets usually write alone in rooms of their own, not with other poets, although there are a few exceptions. The tanka tradition, as the Japanese Imperial anthologies demonstrate, has linked individual poems into longer pieces for over twelve hundred years. It is a small step from editors sequencing anthologies to poets writing tanka with each other. We write differently when responding to another poet than when responding to our inner voices, and sometimes this difference can result in unexpected and moving poems. We have a relational poetic life when we write with another poet.

I have been fortunate to write with two other poets before writing with Autumn. Each time I found the experience creatively stimulating and the poetic relationship meaningful. I wanted to write with someone else, because I wanted to see where another poetic relationship, with its own unique tone, might go. Guess I'm a relational poet.

From our previous correspondence and conversations, I knew Autumn liked birds a lot, as I do, that she played violin, as I still do, and that she was mildly obsessed, if not more so, with our climate crisis, as I am. I felt we could write from a common ground. Also, she is

3

younger than me, and I thought she would bring a mid-life perspective to my older-life-stage view. It was a pleasure to write with her.

As Autumn mentions, I had some rules; well, maybe guidelines. Tanka's link-and-shift, so integral to the form, can lead to large shifts and small links when two people write tanka together. In the Japanese tradition, which Western tanka poets have often emulated, tanka sequences are a journey. Western poems, in contrast, usually have a theme. When the shifts are too large, the poem's theme can easily recede, leaving Western readers, expecting the poem to be about something, puzzled.

I enjoy tanka journeys. I also was curious what responsive tanka might be like if the poets tried to emphasize links over shifts. In retrospect, since our quartets appear in titled sections, rather than as individual sequences, maybe what we've written is a themed journey.

4

coloratura volante

ornamented song in flight

today . . . just in my chair
expectant like those juncos
at the empty feeder
sitting quietly
what I have to offer

one pine needle
floating in the bird bath
true north
winter's silent summons
to the part of me that flies

setting out
on a migration
without a pre-planned route
bringing only a song—
faith there will be supper

not just hunger
that drives us
a longing
to soar wingtip-to-wingtip
on the flyway awhile . . .

an inchworm
measuring the reach
of my writing finger
knows something more of me
than I do

following
the shorebirds' footprints
until they stop
at the tide line
can't remember how to fly

dancing beak-to-beak
with Himalayan gods
Bar-headed geese . . .
this ache beneath my shoulder blades
where wings once were

excavation—
from a carpal bone
reconstructing the skeleton . . .
whatever I discover
is buried within

my childhood window
its hawthorn and cardinal
all gone . . .
but I'll whistle that red song
till the last blossom falls

those Evening Grosbeaks
on the clothes line once
and that focus
on pleasing everyone—
the past still tugs

told that
at two I insisted, "I AM
being-haaave . . . !"
the hunt-and-peck to find
these scattered handfuls of me

a mosaic of beaks
true to size and color
in the gallery
don't think I picked mine
it picked me

dawn-to-dusk birding
swallows in the sun
mergansers . . . falcons . . .
never checked my phone
a sanctuary day

the white dove
hovering above my head
in leaded glass
30 years of penance
the price I paid for peace

twelve-thousand foot pass
dark and darker clouds
instead of pondering
distant peaks
a thunder storm descent

the wild roll
of timpani drums
hailing
a diminuendo
of long-sought sleep

the jack hammer
of a Downy Woodpecker
his love let t t t t t er
about as subtle
as a steel monkey's catcall

the whisper song
of a Stellar's Jay
more intimate than a feather
there's so much to say
beyond lust

how my ears tune
to hummingbird arrivals
Broadtail trill
sometimes the sweetest sound
is simply, I'm home

two emphatic warblers
—first of the season—
we're all migrating
through our years
I'd get lost without companions

Farmer's Market
chard and kale and tangerines . . .
what do I want to do this year?
my internal compass
has its own directions

from the stair landing
there seem only two ways—
up or down
unless one endeavors
to follow Escher's star

back and forth
between light and dark
summer and winter
each day I try to chip
an obsidian spark

orange bellies
where the sunrise should be
a flock of robins
warming this single-digit day
my choice to trek among them

Garden of the Gods
a pair of wild geese alight
atop a pinnacle . . .
but what's even more surreal—
the drone that chased them there

pinged again
can't escape
the digital rifle
we're all big game now
with no place to hide

unable to tame
the wilderness within . . .
instead, we clear-cut
our way through jungle lungs
and suffocate our songs

with peregrine patience
I scan myself for fear
when it shudders
I tear it to pieces
so I can see more clearly

no Calliopes
their magenta rays angling
into sputter-sass . . .
you never know what sweet things
you might have to lose

a hummingbird feeds
as I eat
a plant-based dinner . . .
there are always losses
counting tonight as a win

lifelong Lent—
not just a fast in the wilderness
but for it . . .
what we sacrifice willingly
makes us human, too

more convenient, yes,
but save that open space
the pleasures
of sitting under the oak
even if no birds come

winter chickadees
from tree to feeder all day
I'm busy, too
trying to be less anxious
about my country

carried away
by Smetana's Vltava . . .
my Czech grandmother
immigrated from a place
that no longer exists

now the ballads
about the San Joaquin
lament its dry river bed
name's the same
meaning's changed

iridium layer—
a river of dust that drowned
the dinosaurs . . .
epigenetic destiny,
remains in chickadees

crows, crows, crows, crows, crows
their giddy reunion
grating this time
hard to welcome company
when I need quiet's black

white noise
subdues the happy, happy finch
when my thoughts
start to repeat
I might as well listen

to know why a raven
is like a writing desk
an odd gift
this quill connecting dots
between those thoughts

the riddle's answer
hidden by our tunnel vision
trusting thermals
the leap off the ledge
condor wings expand the view

vacation
birded for a week
watched Lawrence's Goldfinch
bathe in a stream
washed my feathers, too

staycation—
more pollen than polish
to the windows
still, young Western Tanagers
smack into the glass

fledged Cooper's Hawks
scattering crows
—aren't they too big to catch?—
ah, to see more clearly
I'm grown . . . and still trying

yellow flutters
in that far willow . . . wings?
fetching binoculars
I realize the leaves have turned
behind my back

drizzly morning
no birdsong from the hedge
silence
is exactly the sound
I want to hear

an incantation
freezing fog rimes the morning
branch by birdless branch
creations crystallize
in stillness

back from my quest
the wind plugged in
rain snare-drumming the roof
carefully unwrapping
what I found

the chantey
of sea glass held to the light
a bottle song
to fill the white space
of this empty page

col legno

with the wood

a winter tree
reflected in the puddle
even looking at pictures
I can't remember
how I saw myself then

will I know my face
without its ebony frame?
striking
the aspens' silver
against the snow

self-portrait
green-leafed hair
eighth notes for fingers
a bemused smile—
I don't always look like that

though I still see myself
in this pen-and-ink acorn
its plate glass reveals
the red leaves of autumn . . .
when did I become an oak?

the pine's shadow
another way it reaches
the ground
I'm holding onto my friends
to lose less light

all these needles
that shimmered in the morning
fallen
let us gather together
warm ourselves by their fire

that woven basket
a Native American copy
full of kindling—
those tribes that disappeared
what's my link to them?

this broken sherd
of a coil pot, smoothed and sunned
the curve
of the potter's palm
held in mine

lit and tented
the budding cherry tree
glows against the cold . . .
hoping to gather honey
for Rilke's Invisible Hive

compared
to a summer day . . .
well, we're gathering nectar
comb by comb by comb—
same gaze, different vision

mouthfuls of earth
mound between pavers
ant hills . . .
rolling back the stone
from winter's cave

a large snake skin
by the stone wall
—don't we draw each other out?
isn't that how we keep going?—
immortal is a verb

a lone oak
in a twilight silhouette
the shape
of what I have to offer
getting clearer

Ponderosa Pine
I can only wrap my arms
halfway 'round—
hope my love goes farther
than my reach

those crayoned birds
I drew as a kid . . .
the awful knowledge
some limitations
can't be breached

pencil sketches
never quite what I'd pictured
in my mind . . .
my imagination's sky
so limitless

the sweep of the wind
over mountain terrain
sculpting
lenticular clouds
. . . and me

responding
to a birdsong I don't know
climbing the slope
can't follow a path
to what's unexpected

paper quilling
marquise-shaped leaves
in lime green
right around the corner
coiled and waiting—Spring

nubs on the branches
like a musical score
next performance soon
when I can open
the familiar becomes new

a peck
of Evening Grosbeaks
their whistle bleats
like traffic cops
stopping me on the yellow

tomato six-packs
for sale at the market
my soil's not ready . . .
like getting a ticket
for planting late

two clematis vines
climbing the walls inside . . .
spring sleet and snow
force us to yield
force them to bloom

the raised bed's raked
and a jay appears
four feet away
as if I'd planted blue wings
—*avian vegetatus*

new spring leaves
that chartreuse green
warbler trilling
I'm taking pictures
Rashomon effect

bokeh blur
focusing on what we want
to be seen—
a single floret breathes
the lilac's symphony

a floating gardenia
sun lit, shadowed . . . photo-shopped
what I want to shoot
—how we all mirror each other—
won't show up on the film

Talbot's fern fronds—
photogenic drawings'
ethereal glow . . .
the stuff the stuff of life
leaves behind

this meadow
confetti'd with wildflowers
because of beavers . . .
how many bouquets
result from my dams?

after the quake
I'll search the tumbled cupboards
for an unbroken vase
pick some freesias
and redesign the floor plan

like rage
thunderstorms demand their say
writing
lines of lightning
on dark, turbulent clouds

I might paint the sky
with spring rain on a garden
like the old masters—
I'll add a thermometer
climate changed . . . ninety-nine degrees

spoon-fed nutrients—
my plant-by-plant welcome back
to my garden
each leaf-and-bud hello
a word from Mother Earth

even the African Violet
on my desk is flowering
didn't know until now
I'd been holding my breath
for five months

bathing
in this overdue chortle
at robin's panache—
he's making quite a splash
—looks like he'll need a refill

reading Wordsworth's *Prelude*
he gave voice
to rain-sprouted thoughts
and sun-released feelings
—his precipice above us

a bit of bark
on the path I just swept
it seems
there is always more
polishing to do

I want to look
beneath the soil
where the seeds
that volunteered
first grew roots

I don't mind
when they're pointed out kindly
these weeds
maybe help me pull a few
—we'll make a wish for sprouting

a six-foot fence
to keep the deer out
is just the start
how can this garden reflect
the cornucopia I want to be?

ants propagate trillium
—there's a word for that—
for smarty-pants humans
evolution's vampires
we must create one

no peonies
without myrmecophily
plump buds waxed shut . . .
for ambrosial pink perfume
my word to the ants is thanks

like an introduced species
we fill each niche
—fairy lanterns
give way to dandelions—
no enemies . . . except ourselves

the saving grace
of small intentions . . .
dwarf snapdragons
reseed themselves
year after year

a prima vista

upon first sight

sometimes my story
reads like a Greek Tragedy
—all pathos and peplos
but Dionysians would say
if the frowny-face mask fits, wear it

in my story
we need supplies and backup
        to slay the dragon
mission impossible
with just my harebrain?

the best fallback?
a companion along
for the quest
a Sancho P to one's Don Q
—an impossible dreamer

the solitary hero
trudging uphill in the heat
is the real myth . . .
look how far we've come
roped together . . . lots of fuel left

who was it that said,
"I read to make new friends?"
sometimes I'm stuck
in a rock of assumptions
and a book cracks me open

puzzling . . .
no matter how I jigsaw
words into place
the picture they reveal
always turns out to be me

whittling a stick
until it snapped . . . again
that's when I heard the voice
"listen to the wood
it will tell you how to carve"

entanglement
the small talk of particles . . .
sticks and stones
flesh and bone—all star stuff
all in communion

resentment rises
as once more, I bite my tongue
swallowing
the rust-red taste
of a cast-iron moon

lighting the wick
I need a spell
that will stop a worry
from turning
into a rage

quicksilver
some moods accumulate
in the blood
the poisons we swim through
swim through us

the antidote
for what keeps us apart
stares back
from the mirror—
polish more, squint less

a battered childhood
a murdered mom, and yet
no self-pity
just her carry-me-where-you-will
twenty-one-derful laugh

if we could bottle
the stream of well-being . . .
it flows around jagged shards
cools our hot moods
—it can travel uphill

deep underground
a curative aquifer
waiting to be tapped . . .
envisioning my daughter
with that dowsing rod I gave her

the elixir
to salve suffering
only requires
we open the vial
—trying to budge that lid

enduring
the pain of a fracture's
healing . . .
maybe breaking the Soul's bones
knits them stronger, too

"scar tissue," she said
"have to break it up"
—my throbbing heart
at what can't be undone
can calm . . . with practice . . . sort of

underwater
holding my breath
my lungs
pump anyway—hard
to break a habit

a glass swan
its neck as curved
as Taps from a lone trumpet . . .
just our breathing
and what we do with it

a mountain lion
paw-printed last night's snow
below my window
how much of the totem world
stalks by while I am sleeping?

our indoor cat
watches the crow on the wire
tail twitching
despite Buddha, I also long
to reach what I can't

a lynx falls shy
of her snowshoe hare
suffering hunger
how hard to watch others
hitting their marks

a porcelain sphinx
stares at me . . .
the answer to the riddle
how do you stop comparing?
give up

my charcoal trees
lining a mountain lake
don't pop
no art class this week
I search YouTube

drawing on right brains
we turn our magazines
upside down . . .
sketching in Sharpie
erases notions of mistakes

"no color
for the first three years"
said the old masters
the depths of freedom found
in shades of gray

black & white film
tray-to-tray in total darkness
one way
to bring the poetry
of light to life

I rub his belly
and the bullfrog goes to sleep
in my hand
even now, this ability
to still small things

a bale of turtles
swimming towards the shore
to nest
I have to protect them
—and there are predators

how to let go
of wanting to make an impact?
this stack of flat stones
some skip, others sink
the water remains unchanged

I want to repaint
that alpine lake
and frame it—
even better
start another picture

the cranes are back
making plans to go
their guttural call
shivers me open
like a preacher

sometimes, a prayer
for wide wings to lift me
above the slew . . .
other times, for long legs
strong enough to stand

past angst
engaged now with chiaroscuro
and soaring without flapping . . .
not sure what curriculum
got me here . . . except age

so fragile
the hurricane shade
of this old oil lamp . . .
maybe faith protects
that small flame inside

stringendo

an urgent narrowing

on my list
order Beethoven's quartets . . .
I need a life jacket
before kayaking
the daily news channels

toxic waste
streaming from the screens
in our palms . . .
no safety helmet
to shield the brain from 5G

moon viewing
our inheritance
we stop . . . look . . .
show someone how
love can protect us

illuminating
the real . . . the eternal
#aware
not at all the same
as conscious

questions
beneath this melting ice
salamanders—
those who'd wriggle out from under
responsibility

the sheet of science
we walk on
not as thick as we thought
falling through to shiver
where kings shoot messengers

a slippery slope
this climb to the tipping point
we're Sherpas
the fates of so many
on our backs

aquatic fossils
in the mountain top rocks—
which flag to plant
at the summit
hubris or humility?

never mind the garden
an octopus's intelligence
is mostly emotional . . .
how would the researchers describe
us super-primates?

data-based research
leads to left-brained conclusions—
let's ask elephants
how they feel about ivory
and listen for their rumble

feeder full
watching my neighbors, the towhees,
eat their seed breakfast
I like to imagine
they are chinking "thank you"

call it instinct,
intuition, neurons in our guts
we are all fluent
in the universal tongue
of hunger

in my mind's eye
an underwater teeter-totter
grebe down, carp up
bird surfaces, fish dives
—the fulcrum balancing life

recycling center
I toss styrofoam
into the bin
as my first spring swallow
weaves overhead

Pasque flowers
pale blue nectar banks
for hummingbirds—
global warming has changed
their opening hours

when most creatures
live in fenced parks
managed for their protection
will we have saved them?
—Anthropocene *success*

digitalized
in this cult with walls
no place to escape—
out hiking I see
a couple on their cell phones

here—swallowtail—there
till I ask her to land
for a portrait
her wings an open book
—there's just no app for that

don't want to go back
to painting on cave walls
with crushed petals . . .
miss that safe place
that algorithms can't pry

pixel petals
release no perfume
pollen, pheromones
the original WiFi
—nature's sultry come hither

imagine
the last place you felt safe . . .
now tell me—
am I wrong to guess
there wasn't a gun there?

system down
thoughts amok
holding me hostage . . .
those who might help
tied up, too

revolution
not what its cracked up to be
power
to the *wrong* people . . .
still, the purple mountains reign

slogans for me
are thin gruel today . . .
the house was quake-proofed
the tremor stronger
than the foundation could stand

the march
won't impede the president much
this one placard
Daughters of Witches Who Weren't Burned
might

Ground Hog Day
time to read the signs
Get Out of Our Wombs
and face this collective shadow
. . . or nuclear winter

that dream of a fish
leaping high and biting my leg . . .
we came from depths
too dark to fathom—
beware those nature-deprived

an amber pendulum
not swinging side-to-side
—spiraling
we need to reclaim our center
where doctor and healer meet

living
near a fault line
knowing a quake will come . . .
I keep trying to measure
my own micro-creep

I turned down china
for Pennsbury Pottery—
her everyday dishes . . .
random chips and glaze cracks
let Cohen's light get in

heirloom beans
pebble-hard in the market
simmered and softened . . .
I want to pry the sun
out from under my shadow

sand-and-wave honed
the stone in my hand
moon-rounded
tides turn when they will
till we are washed away

grinding bones for bread . . .
John Barleycorn's rise and fall
enacted
at my knife-wielding hands
making mirepoix for our soup

on the stove
masa-thickened chocolaté
if I'd been born
an Inca girl
I might have been sacrificed

blind
to jaguar eyes
today
hungry for profit
we sacrifice the rain forest

splitting
a Tahitian vanilla bean . . .
glad I'll be cremated
at least I'll give
my bones back

this play we're all in
the juggler can't . . .
the king thinks he is . . .
all's not well that doesn't end . . .
and there's no director

fake news? old news
no news is good news
lest we be blinded
best to take a pinhole view
of this media eclipse

hems go down, hems go up
now that we've wired the earth
I notice
my rose colored glasses
are scratched

forget Stage Right or Left
—its curtains for all of us
unless
we realize that this show
must not go on

allargando

broadening, becoming slower

so much forgotten
as if I've been traveling
through dark matter
the memories that mark my passage
months . . . years apart

like a worm hole
the day lily's goblet
warping time—
I'm an Indian maiden
sipping rain from orange cups

my five or six past lives
are all post-partum
the potion
to reveal time's secrets
not yet concocted

chains of paper dolls
all our selves holding hands
maybe we make time
doubling and redoubling
the recipe

four hours round trip
to bring her groceries . . .
two flicker chicks
perched above the suet
awaiting mom's beak full

what to look at?
the feeder . . . the paper . . .
the bubbling spring
arising from that reservoir
we all drink?

the landscape shifts
outside the car window
foreground flying by—
let me be the mountain
everything moves around

mountains moving
just slower . . .
all I possess
is my perspective
—and a set of lenses

spring wind
trees waving like a safety crew
s l o w   d o w n
easy to exceed
the neuron speed limit

clover leaf exits
the triple loops it takes
to get back on track . . .
more time to watch the corn grow
back where I learned to drive

highway, two-lane
back road, no road
—I do like to keep off
the well-traveled trails
of my mind

prairie ruts
where the pioneers pushed
toward new frontiers—
just think of the time it took
. . . and how long they've endured

Slow TV . . .
cruising the Telemark Canal
from my couch
100-year-old lock-and-dams
oddly elevate me

no speed limit
on the digital highway
neon-lit exits
for wildlife viewing
congested before bedtime

hyper-realism
the animator perfects
strands of grass
drawing everything into them
but breath

an empty feeder
through the rain-splatted window
a chickadee lifts . . .
Mary Oliver's wild geese
must be answered each day

dam spillway damaged
and more rain forecast
acting as if I can see
my short-term future
knowing I could be wrong

this delicious day
sunny and warm mid-winter—
yet I'm distracted
thinking about past fires
and the lack of snowpack

the mental jujitsu
required to keep my mind
from distorting my vision
—or does my third eye
let me see beyond myself

to focus outward
or within? no future, past,
self, or other
Grandmother Spider tugs her web
and we dance

unlike a spider
I unwind my thread
to envelop
unwanted intrusions
—only then can I proceed

first flight today
painted lady, mourning cloak
stretching their wings . . .
I like roundtrip adventures
with chrysalis returns

I now walk
the same trail I used to run
doves still cooing
on the great circle route
we're all traveling

the silk of time
woven spoke by spoke
life's dream-catcher
each moment held a moment
before we let it go

cambiare obligato

to change is mandatory

untangling
the long, orange extension cord
again
the current is there
if I can just plug in

throwing up my hands
I recharge on star shine
Orion's belt
each light in working order
. . . unlike this Edison string

thunder storm
and the power's out
glad
the flashlights have batteries
. . . missing my lullaby days

monitor glow
opening my eyes
at 3 am
the refueling station
I am to everyone

can't take it anymore
the bill of goods they hand me
as middleman
trying to keep the peace
tears me to pieces

last month's kerfuffle
replaced by yesterday's
no wonder
we like birds
they can fly away

my great grandpa Max
taught Houdini card tricks . . .
escape acts
not always guaranteed
to keep us from drowning

I've been reborn
a thousand times
not just in daydreams
always bullion in the wreck
if I can find it

imagine
"Will you marry me?" impressed
in the frozen pond's snow . . .
he never did propose
I wore his ring anyway

under the ice
fish wait for the spring thaw . . .
it took me so long to learn
how to descend
and bring back what I needed

neglect accumulates
till I do *becomes* I don't *. . .*
the wake-up call
of a gelid mountain stream
—bracing

a rock slide
closed the opening
of my marriage cave—
dug my way out
with a spoon

just a swipe
of Kilz White
covering over
every inch of my children's
penciled height-lines

two households
not highly recommended
for raising kids
the silence
I could never tune out

no way to take down
the portrait of her dad
my daughter favors
the knight on a white horse
he never did ride

the hole in the wall
behind that faded print . . .
I leave it alone
to remind me
of my limitations

little red wagon
still hauling around
memories
of children who outgrew
my pull long ago

that photograph
of my grandmother . . .
she never reminisced
about the old country
and now she's gone

sorting boxes
of our once-upon-a-time
picture books
trying to hold on
to the best stories

postcards
saved from childhood
that my grandkids don't want
they prefer YouTube videos
and making origami hearts

sorting laundry
our visions worlds apart
I see colors and water temps
he sees his and hers
and yet, we fold together

my books, her orchids
both offer
what can only be grasped
by *oh . . . whoah . . .*
arguing irrelevant

his Wagner, my Bach—
when we cannot agree
to disagree
headphones go a long way
towards quieting things

she plays Grappelli
on the music channel
I play my classical violin
when she walks the dog
—win-win

at the market
she buys beets, he hummus
—both *do* choose avos—
on the way to tomorrow
so many recipes

just a pinch
from the jar marked
"yesterday"
ghost peppers
still make my eyes tear

heirloom seeds
my chance to go back in time
a commitment
beyond success or failure
whether they sprout or not

Dad promised
I could count on them to bloom—
zinnias
colorful as the curiosity
he planted

each caesura
in the owls' elegy
a pause
to reflect on the wisdom
of forgiveness

Rilke's voice
speaking through that archaic torso
to me . . .
what I wished I'd done
and didn't

where is my head . . . ?
life spills out as villanelle
lessons repeat
line by line, and yet
new meaning each time

I can recite
where I lived . . . what I did
—is that person still here?—
it's as if I only exist
when I'm connecting

doloroso

sorrowfully

Sunday morning
something about the light says
call mom
it's been a little while . . .
20 years since she died

my granddaughter hopes to live
to 109 . . .
I'd have a long afterlife
her memory a sun
keeping me in orbit

what is the half-life
of remembering . . . ?
wintergreen
on a moonlit breeze
mom's kiss on my forehead

waking from a nap
disoriented
I'm small . . . overalls . . .
nose-to-nose with violets . . .
I had forgotten

nine years old
"my dance recital's next week
and my teenage brother's weird"
that grandparent prayer
don't let her lose her balance

that clerk who remarked
"it's all just damage control . . ."
surviving teens
somewhere between soft-shoe's tap
and gumshoe's cloak-and-dagger

who did it?
—the clues were everywhere—
we all did
don't need a detective
just a mirror

short of a sprung floor
or a ballet barre
how to soften falls
or spot one another?
Keats held out his living hand . . .

an "excellent candidate"
turned down for lack of experience—
my daughter
drives 40 minutes round trip
to work a single hour

pictures in the album
infant . . . preteen . . . now
the roar of time
drowns our plea
to spare them

hands-on parenting
until it's time to go
hands off . . .
so tough to stand and watch
that bike wobble away

I started to crawl
she baby-proofed the house
now my mom
is losing her sight—
I can't ramp her stairs

leaving the hard backs
she moves into her own life
page by page
the way I helped shape
my daughter's mind

aren't we all writing
our own stories?
—what to put in, what to leave out?—
too many verifiable facts
flatten the narrative

I cast myself
in the supporting role:
mom
now that she's grown, a new play
all our lines, improvised

the actresses rewrite the script
the movie is better
than the book
the director applauds
happy ending

those few
who resonate with me . . .
a silent tuning fork
will sound
when another is rung

they changed the tuning
of their violin strings
—scordatura
as the composer noted—
. . . it's hard to get our inside out

when my brother sang
O Danny Boy *for Dad*
the skies spilled over . . .
even their vast grasp of blue
could not contain such loss

compelled to play
Ashokan Farewell
the melody carries
all the deceased
back to us

the love triangle
of a folded flag
my pledge
allegiance to the soldier
for whom it was retired

memorial wall
I pause at the names of guys
I went to school with . . .
the vet at the off-ramp—
not sure why I don't stop

wearing a gas mask
six channels of Mandarin
blasting my ears
my civilian brother's scoff,
"you've never really served"

protecting us all
so we can work and love
and wish . . .
no defense can stop
a family grenade

he could still sing
that old cowboy song
after dementia
took the chords—
hard to play my break

my banjo-pickin' brother's
foggy mountain breakdown
in my hollows
the strains of our bluegrass days
before he lost his way

the orange-red leaves
stripped by an early storm
looking for a guide
to lead me
through old age

no Pied Piper
in parti-colored clothes
dancing
to this inner voice
playing me home

pensieroso

meditatively

he sang to me
—the dervish in my dream—
of eyes . . .
the way gods look through ours
in order to be seen

personifying
the one great holy spirit
a never-dry well . . .
I kind of miss
when hummingbirds were nymphs

dryads . . .
or mycorrhizal networks?
trees communicate
favoring their children
with rooted wisdom

ear against the wall
of the pantheon . . .
listening
for what's hard to hear
my *raison d'etre*

days to weeks to years
it's not the tide—
a river carries me
no going back, but look
—a kingfisher just plunged

rider of slipstreams
hoarder of bright happenings
a mental magpie, me
soaking in all I can from here
—to that waterfall

the trick
is to gather light and shadow
abracadabra
watch the color swirl
through the mist

it's what we bring back
the minnow from the rill
sustenance enough
to bear witness
to life's magic

cells divide
we individuate . . .
in the parallel universe
our feelers undulate
hoping to touch and recombine

morphic resonance
defining our form . . .
we can grow
to our full potential
or flail phantom limbs

that sixth sense
I know my daughter will call
before she does
the independent self
just an adolescent distortion

eavesdropping
we seek the cosmic hum
just before dawn
when spirit speaks through us
let it be to say good morning

it's a stretch
but I can reach the high notes
I want a contraption
to fling me
beyond the tug of time

a soft touch
on the sweet-spot of the string
harmonics . . .
but even our star won't sing
its solar song forever

on this year's calendar
beneath the open-beaked birds
all those squares
with now-forgotten appointments . . .
I'm evaporating

like the water cycle
little droplets of us absorbed,
reflected by others—
not the calendar's grid
but the seine of Indra's pearls

the colored lights
on my neighbor's trees
like fireworks—
maybe these reading glasses
aren't so bad after all

pushing the baby mouse
back under the bush
I see
I'm now more detached
about what has to happen

a frosty breath
of acceptance
winter's fate
the hare whitens
only her tracks visible

a friend's mom died
reminding me again
where we're going . . .
leaving crumbs
though I'm not coming back

from the edge
that river appears no more
than sparkling ribbon . . .
I thread it between my fingers
let it walk me home

bridge washed out
current too strong to wade
the only way to cross
bushwhack toward the headwaters—
hope the light holds

bramble scratch
and poison ivy blister
a topical map
life-etched on my skin
recalling the way

the territory
can't be digitalized
—each step prepares the next—
impossible to follow
directions to the Acheron

my hero longs for more
time to make a difference
good ol' Jane Goodall
if I could, I'd give her some
of my own

standing on top
of 4.85 billion years
for the length of a wink
wanting to be able to look
the future in the eye

Homo naledi
brought to light from deep inside
the Rising Star caves . . .
perhaps someday the future
might look back at us

clear-cut forests
chimpanzee bones . . . our bones . . .
Bach
hard to piece together
how we disappeared

dayspring hike
we spot a bobcat poised
to catch a rabbit—
even if I knew how
I wouldn't fashion fur hats

don't need
to be a trapper
not sure I want
a virtual reality headset
caught between past and future

this Bristlecone Pine
centuries of winds twisted
into its trunk
a name carved, against the grain
—why can't being be enough?

the *papier-mâché* sculpture
my wife made of our dog
still on the mantel . . .
to have been
is also the question

winter solstice
ads for summer travel
and seed catalogs . . .
the meditation book
touts the present moment

here and now
my fingers fitted to its grooves
this clay pot at once
on my dead parents' mantel
and holding my ashes

a glaze of memories
on the aging urn
firing the kiln
to add the future
as it arrives

carbon markings
of horse hair scribbles
left behind . . .
as yet unbroken, the code
to reign back galloping time

midwinter
soon sparrows and squirrels
at the feeder—
watching the wildlife
as I float down the Styx

cutthroat trout
pooling around a logjam
Yuletide
even in the darkest waters
life holds sway

in the river
trying to grasp
the current
and shape it
with my puny fingers

whitewater whirlpools
roil among the boulders
like questions
of life and death
each shaping the other

wild blueberries
picking a lot—muffins!
eating a few
basket overflowing
with delayed gratification

No Vacancy
guess we'll need another
mason bee hive
—the satisfaction
of hosting a houseful

decoding the buzz
so I can get past
the nectar
not to find god—
companions . . . even sweeter

always
and never alone in this life . . .
I am
each cupful I've swallowed
each cup I've let pass

I look at the sky
and want my pastel box
—connecting the dots
between what I see
and what I can't reach

finding its way
into my pocket
a smoky quartz crystal . . .
little by little
I carry the mountain home

show and tell
the Barn Owl feather
cut from the road kill . . .
I'll keep my hand up
until I get called on

broken, then doubled
the life line on my right palm
all that is
within my grip
* . . . all that isn't*

dal segno al fine

from the sign to the end

gonna call my friend
and catch up
order some more books, too
gonna be like that river
meandering past obstacles

the muddy water
that flooded my childhood
clearing now . . .
it's okay to be backlit
by a Mississippi moon

Proud Mary on the radio
turn it up . . . turn it up
I want to play
with that urgency —
keep practicing, get better

  here
where the pole won't touch bottom
                          there
where the rapids run fast
glad I'm not on this raft alone

at the restaurant
Happy Chinese New Year
a carrot flower on my plate
Frost's two roads
on my mind

only one Tao
one flower, with many names—
no need to choose
between yin and yang
they both bloom within us

twigs in the stream
—will mine float faster?—
as an adult
some of what I do
seems chosen for me

Winnie the Pooh . . .
a willingness to bear
stings for honey
all the been-there-thens
lead to being here now

sun on the frost
noticing I'm noticing
. . . and adding a soundtrack
my endless movie
—trying to give tickets away

I wonder now
if grace is a silent film
maybe
someday I'll erase
these subtitles, too

glad Vermeer
had more than one canvas
still
raked sand art
also necessary

half a century
dabbing at this same
self-portrait
today I sit, naked in snow
white-on-white watercolor

watching moon jellies
—like flowers breathing—
my granddaughter wonders
if they are watching us
get oxygen from air

peering back in time
the chambered nautilus'
great eye
almost as though she knows
we are living fossils, too

tsunami zone
—maybe once a millennium—
after the white-frothed waves
erode my creations
no imprint will be left

what is free will
when the future is known?
to wade in the surf
with children on our shoulders—
to gather shells anyway

up on a ridge
no other houses in sight
birds for neighbors
she teaches herself
to speak seed

I picture an egg
and the vixen relays
my message
each winter morning
her kits at my door

tracks . . .
could be Kinnell's bear—
setting out at last
to find the den
where I can birth

all circle round—
the salmon's swim, the doe's trail
the falcon's reel
the word
for love

Acknowledgements

Our thanks to the following publications for including some of the individual tanka in our connects:

"the chantey" and "a lynx falls shy" appeared in *Cattails*, October 2018

"like rage" appeared in *red lights*, June 2018

"resentment rises" appeared in *ephemerae*, October 2019

"little red wagon" appeared in the *TSA Anthology: Of Love and War and the Life in Between*, Fall 2018

"Dad promised" appeared in *Moonbathing*, Summer 2018

"that clerk who remarked" and "the love triangle" appeared in *Atlas Poetica*, 34, Summer 2018

Cover music : Felix Mendelssohn's
A Midsummer Night's Dream, Scherzo

Autumn Noelle Hall lives and writes in a small cedar cabin in the heart of the Rocky Mountains, where birdsong and Earth song resound. This Nature music— as well as the grief of its impending loss—informs her poetry, which has appeared for over a decade in esteemed journals and anthologies around the world.

David Rice was the editor of the Tanka Society of America's triannual journal, *Ribbons*, from 2012-2019. Any proceeds from his 2019 book, *Pilgrim on the John Muir Trail*, go to support the conservation work of the San Francisco Bay Chapter of the Sierra Club.